To PRA. Leticia
May God Almighty
bless and take good
family: Keep up la Lucha of
love to help reign in the Kingdom
of God among us.

Con mucho cariño y amor,
DR. Pedro G. [illegible] y Santeliz
Greeley Colorado
August 14, 2018 3:17 p.m.

Freedom, Justice, and Love

Dr. Andrés G. Guerrero Jr.

Scriptures taken from the Holy Bible, New International Version®, NIV®. Copyright © 1973, 1978, 1984, 2011 by Biblica, Inc.™ Used by permission of Zondervan. All rights reserved worldwide. www.zondervan.com The "NIV" and "New International Version" are trademarks registered in the United States Patent and Trademark Office by Biblica, Inc.

ISBN: 978-1-4834-8324-5 (sc)
ISBN: 978-1-4834-8323-8 (e)

Library of Congress Control Number: 2018903690

Lulu Publishing Services rev. date: 04/25/2018

To Irma Álvarez Muñiz,
beloved wife of Ramsey Muñiz,
who has never stopped loving, believing, and
fighting for his freedom

He who opens the breach
goes up before them;
they break through and pass
the gate, going out by it.
—Micah 2:13

CONTENTS

For I desire mercy, not sacrifice,
and acknowledgment of God rather than burnt offerings.

—Hosea 6:6

PREFACE

This book is about a man who strived to be the best since his childhood. He is an extraordinary man who demonstrated great love for others throughout his life. Ramsey Muñiz, a spiritual person, became a voice for Mexican Americans, Chicanos, Hispanics, Latinos, and others who lacked representation in politics, and he suffered for it.

Muñiz, a natural-born leader, awakened the consciousness of the sociopolitical, economic, and spiritual needs of the Chicano population in the United States. He was imprisoned for this. Since his imprisonment, nobody has filled this vacuum. We remain grateful for all that he did.

There are various terms used when referring to our people, including Chicanos, Mexican Americans, Hispanics, and Latinos. While I acknowledge and respect the identities embraced by all, this book refers to the Chicano population.

I focus on Chicanos, US citizens whose ancestors are from Mexico. They retain their cultural identity and ancestry despite a world that demands a departure from their native origins. I use the term *Chicano*, and I would be remiss if I did not include the feminine persona. This is uppermost in my mind, knowing that the progress of Chicanos is greatly attributed to the work of women who refer to themselves as Chicanas. Throughout this book, I use the word *Chicano*, and it is inclusive of both Chicanos and Chicanas.

ACKNOWLEDGMENTS

I would like to thank the following people for their contributions and assistance.

Ramsey Muñiz
Dr. Alan Bean
Nancy Bean
Raul G. Garcia
Alberto Luera
Irma Muñiz
Enrique "Kiko" Salazar
Father Harry Sikorski
Charles Chuck Villarreal
Monica Acosta-Zamora

I am thankful for Rev. Paul Jackson, Vicente Velasquez, Jesse Lopez, Oscar Mejia, Trevor Lucas, Brandon Quesenberry, and Judy Robertson for their technical support at Aims Community College.

I also thank Billie J. Bailey and Erin at Octavia Fields Branch Library and Shane at Lone Star College Library for their technical assistance.

We thank all who have provided support, and we are grateful for your love and dedication. On behalf of Ramsey Muñiz and his family, we extend our deepest gratitude to you for providing spiritual and emotional support, giving hope to Ramsey Muñiz and others who struggle to survive in an isolated world. We acknowledge your contributions, knowing that you are the ones who will be welcomed into the kingdom of God.

Oppressors will invariably use their control of sociopolitical power to destroy the credibility of the oppressed's struggle, particularly its leaders.
—*Black Theology and Ideology*

Never abandoning faith

CHAPTER 1

Imprisonment

How does one survive the ongoing pain of imprisonment? Judging by the lengths of prison terms, there are many who do not survive. For them, life ends, or their minds drift to a place from which there is no return. Perhaps this is because prison life is no life. It is merely existing and living in fear, loneliness, and despair.

Most cannot comprehend the pain felt by one whose life has been taken against his or her will. We can only imagine this life and never come close to feeling the anguish of those whose actions are watched and bodies are placed in environments that cause continuous suffering. If imprisonment is so intense, imagine how support from a loved one can provide faith, hope, and love.

Perhaps the greatest pain felt by a prisoner is the inability to be close to family, which in many cases is the only source of love and support. Without families, we are truly alone. If imprisonment is a total separation from one's family in the outside world, the result is negativity, resentment, and, in a sense, the loss of reality.

One might wonder what keeps Ramsey Muñiz alive after all these years of suffering. It all comes down to family. Muñiz's family has never allowed circumstances to cause them to abandon their love for him. They share his physical, mental, and emotional pain, and they support him in every aspect. They are committed to him because they know him to be a loving man, and their love for him is unconditional. It is this same love that we wish for all families who have incarcerated loved ones.

Why is family so important? Sometimes family is all you have. For Muñiz, that is enough. Family was the center of his life, and everything he is today began with family love.

Families are designed to be a cohesive unit. Even though not all families fit the stereotypical definition, people should strive toward maintaining a unity that is at the core of God's plan for human existence. Imprisonment has a devastating effect on this plan. It impacts families and deteriorates the bodies and minds of their imprisoned loved ones. The impact is physical, mental, emotional, and financial. It destroys the bond between inmates and their families, leaving the incarcerated to suffer alone. Spouses are separated from each other, children are left without parents, and grandparents are forced into parental roles through circumstances that are not of their own making.

Families play an important role in healing their imprisoned loved ones, yet physical, mental, emotional, and financial hardships prohibit them from remaining involved in their lives. These hardships are exacerbated by visitation challenges involving distance and time. This sad reality has devastating consequences for all. People of conscience understand this, knowing that we all have a moral obligation to extend love and compassion to those who suffer. Jesus Christ spoke of freeing prisoners throughout his life. If all families with incarcerated loved ones would embrace this mission of love, the suffering of many lives would be lessened.

The support required of families of incarcerated loved ones should not be underestimated. It is immense. It involves financial and emotional support, time, travel, letters, telephone calls, and commissary—all of which come at an enormous cost. These sacrifices impose a great financial burden and in a sense punishment for their having incarcerated loved ones. If healing is to take place for the incarcerated and their families, these burdens should be alleviated. Without this type of reform, our nation will continue to face an increasing number of citizens with mental, emotional, physical, and financial issues.

The unfortunate reality is that family members often become indifferent to the suffering of their incarcerated loved ones. Without nurturing and support from loved ones, the imprisoned suffer without dignity, purpose, or a sense of belonging to the human race. This results in hopelessness, illness, mental deterioration, and death, while families in the outside world remain oblivious to their suffering.

There are many people like Ramsey Muñiz who have been imprisoned for circumstances rather than guilt. They are victims of a flawed legal system that makes it impossible to prove their innocence. We must advocate for the type of change that will end the ongoing suffering for people in these situations. In essence, we have a moral obligation to support all who suffer.

We encourage leaders to research the devastating impact that imprisonment has on society. It represents ongoing suffering, lost relationships, and sadness that oftentimes cannot be overcome. Whose job is it to study the effects of incarceration on our society? Perhaps a department should be established for such an undertaking. For the reader who says, "This is their problem," little do they understand that from a moral standpoint, suffering should be everyone's problem. From a mental health point of view, ongoing suffering impacts the mind, and brings about expressions of anger and resentment. Those who have suffered incarceration become the free citizen of tomorrow.

Arise, shine, for your light has come,
and the glory of the Lord rises upon you.
See, darkness covers the earth
and thick darkness is over the peoples,
but the Lord rises upon you
and his glory appears over you.

—Isaiah 60:1–2

Photographs of Ramsey Muñiz and Family

CHAPTER 2

History of Ramsey Muñiz

Ramiro "Ramsey" Muñiz was born on December 13, 1942, in Corpus Christi, Texas. Translated into English, the words *Corpus Christi* mean the "body of Christ." Eucharistically and linguistically, the name of the city has spiritual significance. It has political roots in that Corpus Christi is the city in which two national organizations were founded—the League of United Latin American Citizens (LULAC)[2] and the American GI Forum.[3] The city of Corpus Christi is a fitting birthplace for Ramsey Muñiz, who is remembered for his spiritual nature and for helping his fellow man through politics.

Ramsey Muñiz is the second of five sons born to Rudy G. and Hilda Longoria Muñiz. His father worked as a mechanic to support the family, while Hilda raised their sons with such immense love that she made them feel rich even though they were poor. It was her love that motivated Muñiz to excel. She taught him to be proud and to be the very best in all that he did. In speaking about his mother, he remembers that she would tell him to show the world who he was and let them know the man that she brought into this world. Muñiz carried his mother's words in his heart and embraced her love in everything that he did.

There were never complaints about hard work. All the boys

understood the need to help the family. Muñiz began working at a young age, and hard work remained a part of him throughout his life. One might wonder how a child could be motivated to engage in such hard work. Muñiz was driven by the love that he had for his mother and family.

Among the earliest jobs that Muñiz did as a boy was to work in the fields picking cotton. He and his brothers worked with their mother to help the family make ends meet. The labor contractor's truck carried them all, young and old. They took sack lunches, wearing long-sleeved shirts, khakis, jeans, handkerchiefs, and straw hats. Women wore scarves to protect their necks and faces from the sun. Seeing his mother work in such conditions made Muñiz work nonstop and submit the heaviest loads of cotton. In the end, he would give her his wages, intent on contributing to the family's well-being.

Around the age of thirteen, Muñiz became a paperboy in Corpus Christi, Texas. He was determined to customize his service by throwing the paper skillfully, making it land by people's front doors. He became so successful that eventually he and his brother Rudy had the largest paper route in the city. This enabled them to purchase a jeep solely for their newspaper route, which began at four o'clock every morning and finished in time for Muñiz to make his way to school.

Additional employment opportunities eventually presented themselves, and Muñiz was given a job of setting pins at a bowling alley. After football practice, he would go home to grab a sandwich that he would eat while setting pins. He was so quick that people would ask for the lane that he worked. After ten o'clock, he was driven home so that he could rest and be up at four o'clock to resume his paper route. In spite of the hard work, Muñiz excelled academically and in all that he did.

While in high school, Muñiz was dropped off one summer in Victoria, Texas, where he would refuel eighteen-wheel trucks. He was to do this work throughout the summer, so his father had a rented room in which he would stay. The apartment was a couple of miles from the work site, so Muñiz would rise early and run a couple of miles so that he could be there before the trucks were to arrive early in the morning.

Muñiz would return home from work in the afternoons. Eventually, he began to ask neighbors if he could mow their lawns. He provided such quality work that he gained the respect of those who paid for his services. They would feed him and extend kindness to a young man whose work ethic they greatly admired.

Hard work was a way of life for Muñiz, a young man who willingly gave his wages to his mother, knowing that it would help the family. His will and determination to succeed were part of his character from a very young age, and he was loved for being the person that he was.

Devotion to family, love, and hard work were not the only things that characterized Muñiz. He had a beautiful heart, and he demonstrated love for others. When he was about five years of age, his grandmother Rosa would ask him to accompany her on healing missions. There were five brothers, yet she would always ask him for reasons that only she knew. Perhaps it was because of his drive to succeed and help others.

Muñiz followed his grandmother, carrying her bag of herbs, images, and candles. He learned that prayer was central to the ability to heal. Muñiz would watch her place a photograph and candles by a statue of La Virgen de Guadalupe. He witnessed her making the sign of the cross on the foreheads of the ill and reciting the rosary. At the end, she would ask him to place his hands on the infirm and pray, believing that God would hear the prayers of an innocent child. He would pray as instructed, asking God for a healing. The infirm would return days later, bringing food in gratitude for their prayers.

Grandmother Rosa lived to be 104. To this day, she comes to her grandson in dreams. She communicates with him spiritually, providing medical care and love that he can feel from a place he does not know.

Like all others, Muñiz faced challenges throughout his life. One of his greatest challenges was overcoming a stuttering problem that he acquired as a child. His stuttering was so severe that it was difficult for others to understand what he was trying to convey. When he was to make his First Holy Communion, the nuns ran him out, believing that he was making fun of the prayers he had been asked to recite.

During his junior high school years, the stuttering continued, yet it did not keep Muñiz from striving to succeed. One day, he announced that he would run for student council president, surprising teachers and students alike. On the day he was to deliver his campaign speech, the students assembled, expecting to hear the stuttering of a boy who struggled to speak. When his time to deliver a speech arrived, Muñiz prayed and asked God for help. He approached the podium and delivered a flawless speech, bringing everyone to their feet to applaud his faith, will, and courage. He demonstrated these qualities as a boy, and they remained a part of him throughout his life.

Muñiz continued to work on his speech impediment through speech therapy and using the power of prayer. He prayed unceasingly, asking God to remove his stuttering. One night, he had a dream in which he was told that he would be well. Believing that he would be healed, he woke up to tell his mother and grandmother about the dream, and he did so without stuttering. When they heard him speak, they screamed with joy and immediately fell to their knees to thank God for the miracle they had witnessed.

During his high school years, Muñiz became known for excelling in the sport of football. He acquired such skill that he gained the respect of many. He strived to be the best and encouraged other members of the team to do the same. Pride was a quality that his mother had instilled in him since his childhood. Muñiz strived to be the best in the sport, and he did so out of love for his mother.

Muñiz became involved in seeking equal representation, knowing that there were no African American cheerleaders. Being a successful football player, he took the position that it was time for them to be included. He and others agreed to vote for an African

American, knowing that the administration had not previously selected a minority. The football players threatened a student walkout, which would leave the school without a team. As a result, administrators recounted the ballots to ensure that they had been properly counted, and Roy Miller High School elected the first cheerleader of color in its history.

Pete Ragus, Muñiz's former Miller High School coach, has written about Muñiz's character and skill, stating,

> I have been a coach and athletic director in Texas for thirty-seven years. I am presently retired. During that thirty-seven-year period, I have had the opportunity to work with many fine young men. Ramsey was one of the finest young men I had the privilege of coaching. In becoming an outstanding athlete and securing a law degree, he overcame so many difficult obstacles that it seems unbelievable that he accomplished what he did. I have never known a more dedicated and hardworking young man. He had an unyielding faith and determination to accomplish what appeared to be impossible things. During all that time I worked with him, his honesty and integrity were above reproach.

Hilda Longoria Muñiz, Ramsey Muñiz's mother, was known for her kindness, love, and valor. The love she had for her sons helped Muñiz excel in all that he did. She instilled courage and strength and her expectations of him letting the world know who he was.

Muñiz became an extraordinary athlete and he was awarded a four-year scholarship to Baylor University—one of the top five universities in Texas. He was fierce on the football field, yet most did not realize that his strength was due to the immense love he had for his mother. He was intent on being the best that he could be, so that she would take pride in a son she had brought into this world. Muñiz was also dedicated to his studies. Because of his academic achievement, he was subsequently accepted into Baylor Law School.

Muñiz had noble goals that he would pursue upon completion of his law degree. "My goal is to be a lawyer. So many people have helped me out. I want to help people out who haven't had the opportunity" (Abernethy 1966).

While he was studying at Baylor University, Muñiz learned that his mother had become gravely ill. With almost no money, he hitchhiked to Corpus Christi, Texas, and arrived in time to hold her during her last moments. Hilda Longoria Muñiz died at the age of forty-two. During the funeral home services, Muñiz stood beside her and remained there all night to ensure that she would not be alone as she made her transition to heaven.

After finishing law school, Muñiz aspired to run for the Texas Board of Education, hoping to promote classes in multicultural education and the history of Mexicans in Texas. He hoped to break monopolies and increase taxes for corporations so that they would better serve society. He spoke of the needs of minorities, hoping to change long-held perspectives about them.

For the most part, minorities were not included as members of the Democratic and Republican Parties. Their votes were sought during elections, but they were excluded from the political system that governed everyone's way of life. The Raza Unida Party, an independent political party, eventually came into existence.[1] The party brought the consciousness of human need to the forefront, voicing the needs of the less fortunate in sociopolitical, economic, and educational matters. Education, employment, health care, child development, and care for the elderly were among the issues that pertained to common people.

The Raza Unida Party was comprised of college youth and others who became involved in politics to represent Chicanos, Mexican Americans, and others who sought a better way of life. The party followed the democratic process and found candidates to represent them in local elections, and they were successful. Incumbents were losing their long-held positions to candidates of an independent political party. Eventually, the party sought a candidate who would run for governor. At the age of thirty, Muñiz ran for governor of Texas in 1972; he ran again in 1974.

Although Muñiz did not win the 1972 or 1974 gubernatorial election, the numbers who turned out to vote for him were astounding, and this was partly due to his ability to speak. He would draw huge crowds because people loved to hear what he had to say. They were motivated by a charismatic person who spoke from his heart. Muñiz could communicate with people, because he understood the needs of the less fortunate, having experienced a hard life of economic struggles with his family. He was intelligent, energetic, and truthful, and his ability to motivate people scared the establishment.

Ramsey Muñiz was invited to speak at most major universities throughout the country. In the West, he spoke at every leading university from Washington State University all the way down to the University of Texas. In all, he spoke in more than twelve states. In the East, he was well received at leading Ivy League universities, including Harvard, Princeton, and Yale. When he spoke at universities, he often received standing ovations from capacity crowds that were comprised of students, faculty, and professionals.

Muñiz spoke of political representation, culture, family, freedom, and justice for Chicanos, Mexican Americans, and others. Today he speaks of family, spirituality, and love—not only for our people, but for humanity, reinforcing the dignity of all.

Having met Muñiz and learned about the man that he was, I felt the need to ask what drove him to become involved in politics. As a successful young attorney who graduated from Baylor Law School, he certainly had no need to enter the world of politics. I asked him why he ran for governor. In his reply, he described having witnessed politics in his neighborhood and having studied politics in school. Muñiz had never seen a Chicano, a Mexican American, or a person of color included in the political process and wondered if those in politics were just not aware of them. Eventually, he came to the conclusion that people were intentionally excluded for reasons that only the establishment could answer.

When I think of the contributions that Muñiz and members of the Raza Unida Party made, the words *change* and *inclusion* come to mind. All people want to be included in matters pertaining to positive change and progress in their lives. Unfortunately, prejudice and intolerance often keep this from happening.

The Raza Unida Party gave life to people who wanted to become actively involved in the political process. Members followed the political process just as other independent political parties do today. In many respects, the party brought about new thinking and change. Sadly, this became a threat to those who did not support change and inclusion.

Because of his political involvement, the establishment set about to imprison Muñiz. It found a way to set him up several times, to attack his character, and to make the public believe that he was involved in criminal activity and conspiracies to distribute drugs as a means of obtaining wealth for personal gain. In my eyes, nothing could be further from the truth.

The first indictment for a conspiracy to import marijuana took place in 1976, after Muñiz had run for governor of Texas twice. As a successful criminal defense attorney, Muñiz defended clients who had been charged with criminal offenses, including those that involved drugs. During the 1976 trial, a former client of Muñiz's, who was incarcerated, was brought to court so that he could testify against him. The witness testified that Muñiz had knowledge of his illegal activities. This testimony brought about Muñiz's conviction; he was indicted for a marijuana conspiracy charge in two different courts (the Western District in San Antonio, Texas, and the Southern District in Corpus Christi, Texas). It was counted twice, and in a later 1994 case that was added to those two, he received a sentence of life without parole.

During the 1976 case, the media convicted Muñiz publicly, ensuring that there would be no doubt about his guilt. Others, however, felt that the public had not heard the entire story. Muñiz, a frightened young attorney with no criminal history, fled to Mexico when he was told that the government was pursuing him. He was captured and sustained the hardest physical consequences before being brought back to face trial. Muñiz was told that leniency would depend on his cooperation and providing information about the Raza Unida Party. Knowing what this meant, he pleaded guilty, to avoid bringing hardship to his friends and family. He was eventually tried, convicted, and sent to various prisons throughout the country.

Muñiz pleaded guilty on the advice of his attorney, having been told that they were out to get him. More importantly, he pleaded guilty to fulfill the terms of a plea agreement, and combine the two conspiracy charges into one case as agreed by all, but this did not happen. While some might pass judgment for his pleading guilty, nobody can understand decisions that are made under duress. The fact is that nobody was in Muñiz's situation—not even those who benefitted from his efforts.

Shortly after his release from prison, Muñiz encountered another legal problem. While living in Dallas, Texas, he established himself as a legal assistant for a law firm. He went to Houston to meet a potential client at his apartment. The apartment was suddenly entered by law enforcement when the potential client left briefly for the store, asking Muñiz to wait. According to Muñiz, they found nothing on him and searched the apartment, stating they had found a tiny amount of cocaine at the top of a closet. Muñiz was charged, and court documents revealed an amount of 0.28 grams. Feeling dejected and unable to change his situation, Muñiz pleaded no contest to the charges. The drug distribution charge was subsequently dismissed by an appellate court due to an illegal search and seizure. Because he traveled out of Dallas County, however, he had violated parole, and was returned to prison for two years.

For the most part, Muñiz lived a quiet life after the 1976 convictions. He was recently asked why he never contacted former members of the Raza Unida Party after he was released from prison. He stated, "I did not want to hurt them. I knew what it was like to be persecuted."

The last conviction of Ramsey Muñiz was in 1994, after he had been happily married for nearly a decade. While he was working as a legal assistant, law enforcement agents followed him and stopped him without reason. They opened the trunk of a car he had been asked to move and found cocaine. The Criminal Complaint stated the reasons used to stop Muñiz, and those reasons were proven to be false by witnesses at the trial. Information that would have exonerated him was withheld until the jury was about to deliberate. By then, it was too late, and Ramsey Muñiz was sentenced to life without parole.

When one thinks of Muñiz's character and what he accomplished politically, one can understand why he was pursued and repeatedly convicted. Elected officials, political incumbents, law enforcement, prosecutors, judges, and business owners did not like the political changes that came about through his leadership and the movement of an independent political party. He was convicted for drug-related crimes and labeled as a criminal. This was a tragic end for one who had been at the forefront for his people. There is great injustice in this.

Muñiz represented the needs of the underprivileged; he is imprisoned for life because of this—and not for a violent or murderous act. He has never been a violent man. On the contrary, he is a good man, an advocate for people, and a defender of justice.

Today, Muñiz remains imprisoned for life. This is a great price to pay for one who had intentions of helping his fellow man. In spite of his suffering, his love for others remains steadfast. Chains may imprison his body, but he has never abandoned the love in his heart or his faith in God.

The ongoing imprisonment of Muñiz is political and unjust. Spiritual consequences will be felt by those who have known this yet have never provided assistance. God's ways eventually touch the lives of all in ways we cannot predict. The need to provide assistance lies with each of us, especially our country's leaders.

They are the ones with the power to change this tragedy. As Pope Francis has stated, "A political society endures when it seeks, as a vocation, to satisfy common needs by stimulating the growth of all its members, especially those in situations of greater vulnerability or risk."[4] Nobody is at greater vulnerability or risk than one who sacrifices his life for the sake of others.

I needed clothes and you clothed me, I was sick and you looked after me, I was in prison and you came to visit me.

—Matthew 25:36

Long Road for a Visit

CHAPTER 3

Importance of a Visit

When my son, Andres, found information about Ramsey Muñiz, he called me to tell me what he had learned about his unjust conviction. I read the information and made the decision to visit him in the US penitentiary in Leavenworth, Kansas. My goal was to give him moral support, which I do to this day. After seeing him and knowing what I do about his history, I have no doubt that his incarceration is political.

There is nothing more gratifying than visiting Muñiz, who is an extraordinary man. He exemplifies the God-given qualities of freedom, justice, and love in everything that he says. More important, he demonstrates these qualities in all that he does for his fellow man. There are few people who possess such a noble character, and Muñiz is certainly among them. Those who visit him understand the beautiful man that he is.

The importance of a visit can never be overestimated. When he sees me, Muniz's great smile expresses happiness. He is grateful and appreciative of a visit. You see these same emotions from other prisoners whose families visit them. They travel from different parts of the United States to see their loved ones who are incarcerated. Some are there for a few months, and others are there for many years. In Muñiz's case, it is life without parole.

During the visit, Muñiz is energized as he teaches me about the purpose of life, which is love and compassion for our fellow man. He is a prophetic and powerful messenger for God. One might say that he is the incarnation of freedom, justice, and love—three powerful elements found in both the Old Testament and the New Testament. People like Muñiz give me reason to live with a spiritual purpose. He inspires me to be the very best—not only for myself, but for the sake of all humanity.

One of my first visits took place on Saturday, September 30, 2006. I traveled to visit Muñiz in Florence, Colorado, and I waited two hours to see him. There was a delay because my name had been associated with the visitors of an inmate named Nuñez. After an hour, a young guard asked whom I was waiting to see. When I told him, he confirmed that Muñiz was the person I was to visit. The guard called for him and was very apologetic about the mistake. An hour later, Ramsey came out, along with two other young inmates, who went on with their visitors. Muñiz and I shook hands and embraced each other. We sat and began to talk, as we were both happy to finally meet each other.

Muñiz had been transferred to Florence, Colorado, after being in an institutional hospital in Springfield, Missouri, where he recuperated from gallbladder surgery and complications that arose. He almost died after surgery, and he spent eight months not only trying to get well but reflecting on a near-death experience (NDE) that changed him for the remainder of his life. He lay weak and motionless after surgery. When he opened his eyes, he saw that he was near the ceiling, which was many feet above the floor. He felt that he was lying on a spring mattress, which surrounded only his body. He was too scared to look to the side, fearing that he would fall many feet down. Suddenly, a bright light filled the room. Muñiz glanced down and saw a light that shined from his body by the ceiling all the way down to the body lying motionless on the bed. Muñiz slowly descended into his physical body. As the two bodies merged, his energy was renewed. It was then that he knew he would live. Little did he know, however, that other spiritual encounters would continue throughout his life—to this day.

Through the grace of God and presence of his wife, Muñiz got well and was subsequently transferred to Florence, Colorado, where our visit took place. During the visit, we talked about his case, personal events, and people that we knew. He spoke of reading ancient Nahuatl texts and explained the origin of the word *Mexican*. The word, broken into parts, means "people of God" in Nahuatl. He defined the word linguistically and in the context of a world that existed in our ancient culture.

We spoke of people who demonstrate hatred because of a lack of love of themselves. Muñiz spoke of the devastating consequences of self-hatred, which many suffer at an early age because they do not know the beauty of their ancestry. Self-hatred is manifested by many who are violent, such as those who kill. Such hatred exists among the imprisoned, and it continues to grow in the free world. The reason for this is that the world is greatly lacking in spiritual growth.

Every time I visit Muñiz, I am reminded that he demonstrates spirituality in all that he says and in everything that he does. Ramsey Muñiz is a beautiful soul. He is a good man with an ability to lead for the sake of helping others. He is a spiritual healer and a true humanitarian who demonstrates love of self and love for others. He knows that to have love for others, one must first possess love of self. When one has self-love, one cannot hate, for to hate others is to hate oneself. He also understands that true love cannot be compromised, even in matters of injustice and inequity.

During our visit, I purchased food from vending machines. As I was opening the package, Muñiz said, "Let's give thanks to God."

We prayed, and I treasure these moments as a spiritual gift from one who suffers. I always pray before I eat. While I had forgotten to do so, Muñiz had not. I was reminded that I was in the presence of a human being who, despite great suffering, maintains faith and love for God.

Dear children, let us not love with words or speech but with actions and in truth.

—1 John 3:18

Thoughts, Hopes, and Dreams

CHAPTER 4

Letters and Writings from Within

I have gained an appreciation for Ramsey Muñiz through the thoughts that he expresses in his letters. They are beautiful, insightful, and profound. I share excerpts of the letters so that the reader will see this man through my eyes. I have received hundreds of letters from Muñiz, and they cover a broad range of topics. The most prevalent are suffering and spirituality. His words are so compelling that they reinforce my belief that his incarceration is political and unjust.

I began to receive letters from Muñiz in 2004, a time in which he had been in solitary confinement for two years. His writings reflected his research on our ancient history. He studied history to learn more about his identity and find meaning in suffering. I have kept a hundred or more letters in which Muñiz addresses topics that include spirituality, freedom, prayer, family, and faith. Each letter has a message that merits analysis for its profundity.

Muñiz's harsh captivity has been physical, yet spirituality has sustained him throughout his years of incarceration.

The following are excerpts of letters that I have received from Ramiro Muñiz throughout the years.

Spirituality

It was during this mode of darkness, that I learned about our ancient spirituality of liberation, justice, and desire for Aztlan, our ancestral place. I dedicated every second, minute, and hour of the day to the intellectual enlightenment of the present and, most important, the truth of our glorious ancient past. It was then that I found the profound reasons that oppressors throughout history did not allow us to seek the essence of who we truly are.

Struggle for Freedom

Subconsciously, without communicating or even writing about it, our struggle for freedom has always been a spiritual one, because world history from the beginning of creation has revealed this. This is especially true knowing that God sent His son, Jesus Christ, into this world to bring freedom, justice, faith, conviction, pride, discipline, and, most important, the true meaning of love.

Families

We must begin to take care of our families. We are no longer strangers or enemies of each other. Some prefer to call themselves Chicanos, Hispanics, and Latinos. That is fine for now, because soon we will all return to who we are from the birth of our own creation as a race, as a nation, and as a people.

Hours in Prayer

I have been praying and meditating for at least three hours or more. I have devoted my life to God, Jesus Christ, and nuestra Virgen de Guadalupe. There is no question that they also need me as I need them, because through me they will be able to demonstrate to the world that even though one can be chained, shackled, oppressed, hungry, lonely, sad, and in darkness, there is always the light of God that shines in one's life to seek freedom, justice, and love for humanity and to always bring forth forgiveness.

The Power of Prayer in Suffering

There is no question that I am going through heavy emotional experiences and changes like never before in a long time, to the point that my mother, Hilda, embraced me last night. We both cried together, because she understands how I feel especially after such drastic and oppressive imprisonment that is unlike others. She shares that it is very difficult for those in the free world—even those close to my heart and soul—to know the suffering and pain that I have had to endure and continue to endure to this very day without complaining or feeling sorry for myself. The only thing that has been difficult for me has been to hold my tears back, but our father, Dr. Salvador Álvarez, has shared that even Jesus Christ had tears from his heart and soul. Those tears do not come from weakness but from the love that one possesses in his heart and soul. My mother, Hilda, made sure that I did not ask others to feel sorry for me but to pray so that I would overcome such hurt, pain, suffering, and sadness.

From Near Death to Forgiveness and Love

How can I ever forget those days of hunger, thirst, cold, darkness, and being naked while in chains and shackles for days, weeks, and months? For the longest time, I was ready to give up my life, asking God to please take me because I could no longer take this suffering. I was almost skin and bone, and on that very special day that I was on my knees, I could feel the presence of Jesus Christ, my beloved brother and Savior, who had suffered and was imprisoned, who was constantly beaten, who was naked in the hole, and who was finally taken out of the hole and nailed alive by his hands and feet to the cross of suffering, forgiveness, and love. As I suffered, He came into the cell and told me to rise and let the oppressor and the world know who Ramsey Muñiz really was and shall be forever. You cannot imagine how I felt. I rose from my knees and began to shout as loudly as I could, "Freedom, freedom, and freedom!"

The prison officers came to my cell and asked me if I was all right. I said that I had never ever felt better in my entire life. I began smiling and laughing and even gave a two-step dance for the joy that my heart felt, because it was full of forgiveness and love" (Ramiro Muñiz, personal communication, 2016).

Houses and wealth are inherited from parents,
but a prudent wife is from the Lord.

—Proverbs 19:14

Irma with Parents and Irma and Ramsey

CHAPTER 5

A Wife's Perspective

The hardship I have faced since my husband's 1994 trial has given me reason to reflect on the man that I married. I met him at a gathering of friends in Dallas, Texas. I knew he had experienced problems, yet little did I know the depths of the suffering he had known. Rather than speaking of past experiences, he demonstrated love. That love continues to define the man that he is today.

I am the daughter of the late Dr. Salvador Álvarez and the late Irma Ramos Álvarez. Both of my parents were educators, and my father was one of the first bilingual education doctoral professors in the Texas education system. They loved Ramsey as much as he loved them.

When I married my husband, I did not realize the essence of his heart. I could not adequately describe the beauty in one who has pride, courage, intelligence, dignity, compassion, spirituality, and love. Everything that he does is motivated by love, and he is known for giving all that he has to help others. This is who he is, and I did not understand the profoundness of his character until he was imprisoned. To this day, I thank God for giving me a most beautiful man whose life, beliefs, and love embody all that God seeks of every human being. I know that my husband has received miraculous blessings for being the man that he is, and I thank God for blessing me through him.

I met my husband around 1983, and I knew that he had previously been incarcerated. I married him believing that despite his past we would live a beautiful life, and we did. He is a loving man who demonstrates great dedication to family. In 1994, ten years after we were married, our lives suddenly changed. The following is a summary of what took place.

Ramsey worked as a legal assistant. As he was about to fly home from working in Houston and Dallas, he was pursued by law enforcement. He was arrested and subsequently convicted for a drug-related offense. I remember receiving a brief telephone call in which he let me know that he had been arrested. He said, "Don't worry. There has been a mistake." I was devastated to hear these words, not knowing what happened. Little did I realize that he himself did not know what had happened.

In March 1994, while working in Dallas and Houston, Ramsey met a potential client who was seeking an attorney. The man asked him to move his car to a different motel where he would continue to stay. While driving the car, Ramsey sensed that he was being followed by an unmarked police car. Because of his past experiences, he knew the signs. He quickly parked the car and walked briskly toward a public phone so that he could call an attorney. Fear and suspicion about the car he had been asked to move raced through his mind. As vehicles were surrounding him, he thought, *If I throw the keys, it will be perceived as guilt. If I give the keys to them, it will be giving consent to search a car I was just asked to move.* Without an alternative, he placed the keys in his sock. He never made it to the phone, and the keys were eventually found. He was searched without his consent, and cocaine was found in the trunk of the car.

The trial that was held in Sherman, Texas, revealed the following: Ramsey's fingerprints were *not* on the cocaine or in the car he had been asked to move. Although there were fingerprints in the car, the government did not disclose the identity of the person whose fingerprints they were. After the trial, the government destroyed the cocaine and retired the dog that had alerted them to the trunk, having admitted that the dog was not trained to detect cocaine and had failed certification prior to this case. The dog was also known for making false-positive alerts.

The reasons used by agents who pursued Muñiz were proven to be false by witnesses. In the Criminal Complaint, it was stated that hotel employees had contacted agents because of suspicious activity, such as making too many telephone calls from the lobby. During the trial, the employees testified that nobody had contacted them and that there was no suspicious behavior. The defense accounted for all phone calls made from the lobby as being family calls or calls for business-related purposes. At one point, the defense asked the court which of the calls were allegedly made for drug business. The response was "We do not have to tell you." Since the transcript proved there were no fingerprints, weapons, or money involved, who would accept such questionable evidence?

In a subsequent chapter, Dr. Alan Bean refers to the trial testimony of an unidentified man's statement overheard by a single agent—one of three who were listening. The agent said that an unidentified man speaking with Muñiz had stated that he did not know them very well, but he would make a deal at ten. The words spoken by the unidentified man were in Spanish. Of the three agents who had heard, only one of them spoke Spanish. From this thirty-minute conversation, which the agent stated was totally in Spanish, the agent could recall only one sentence. It was a statement made by the unidentified man, who was approached by agents at the airport prior to his release. Ramsey Muñiz was convicted based on one statement by a man who neither testified nor was cross-examined by the defense. Again, who would want a family member convicted on evidence such as this?

Throughout the trial, Ramsey struggled to understand what had happened. He could not have known, as information was withheld by the prosecution. It was not until the jury was about to deliberate that exculpatory material was briefly shown to the defense. The documents revealed that government agents were pursuing a man who had made a drug deal with an undercover agent, and the name Ramsey Muñiz was *not* on the report. The man they were pursuing was Medina, the potential client who had asked Muñiz to move his car. They approached him at an airport and allowed him to leave rather than taking him into custody and bringing him to trial as a material witness.

My husband is serving a sentence of life without parole because of two previous convictions made while he was involved in politics. During his career as a successful attorney in 1976, he was indicted on a marijuana conspiracy charge. Indictments were made in two different cities and in two different jurisdictions, yet they were less than six months apart. Ramsey pleaded guilty and signed a plea agreement on the advice of his attorney, so that the two indictments would count as one. The plea agreement was agreed to and signed by lawyers on both sides, but it was later considered invalid because even though the judges in the two jurisdictions had agreed, they both died before their signatures were obtained in a timely manner. In 1994, the two indictments remained as two and his sentence was enhanced to life without parole under the Three Strikes law.

My husband may be classified as a "career criminal," but we who know him understand that he is anything but this. An eighteen-year-old conviction does not indicate recidivism and should not have been used to enhance his sentence to life without parole.

Wrong perceptions, mistakes, biases, and wrongful actions impacted my husband's convictions and resulted in incarceration for life, and this should never have happened. I say this believing that my husband was framed in the 1994 trial. I also believe that he was innocent of his previous convictions. His conviction in 1976 came during a time when political change forced the inclusion of poor people who had no political voice. There was resentment by the wealthy, who saw this change as a disadvantage. Some who had been associated with my husband felt fear and anger.

They were convinced of his guilt through media coverage, court proceedings, and my husband's decision to plead guilty. Most did not communicate with him throughout his subsequent years of imprisonment. Other than his ties to family, he suffered in prison alone. Others were harassed for seeking freedom and justice.

My husband has been incarcerated for more than thirty years throughout his life, and his pain has been unjust; he has suffered like no other. This represents many years of cruel and unusual punishment, which has impacted family members who suffer with him.

People may wonder how love can exist in spite of having experienced so much sadness. I recall the life that I once had with my husband prior to his incarceration. We shared ten beautiful years of happiness. He was a family man who demonstrated great love toward me and our families. He treated my parents with respect. When my father passed away, we moved home to Corpus Christi, Texas, so that we could be close to my mother, who was a central figure in our lives.

When Ramsey was arrested in 1994, I understood how great his suffering was. We had lived a beautiful married life, and there was nothing but goodness in his heart. I refused to allow the circumstances and actions of others to destroy the love that we had shared, knowing that my abandoning him would condemn him to suffering for the rest of his life. Such a decision would ensure everything but happiness in my own life, so I made the decision to focus my time and energy on bringing him home.

I have suffered for twenty-four years, having been denied the presence of my husband. My entire family has suffered with me, yet they continue to support my efforts to free him. I am grateful for this, and I thank God for the love and unity that we share.

I was born into a family that believes in love. We were raised to love, respect, and forgive one another. Without my family, I would not be the person I am today. Having witnessed my suffering and the suffering of my husband, they could have encouraged me to abandon him, but they never did. Instead, they assist me in my efforts to give him my ongoing support. I will always love them for this enormous gift of love.

We are supported by many people who demonstrate love for my husband. They have remained with us for many years, supporting our efforts to free my husband. We owe our lives to them, and we will always pray for their well-being. I believe that they are favored by God for the love they have extended to us and many others.

We are all born into circumstances and experience events in our lives yet we do not understand why. Only God can understand the love-filled purpose in our lives. While our purpose remains unknown to us, one thing is certain. Love gives life, and it is love that sustains it. Knowing this, we are expected to give courage, strength, and life to others, and this is especially true of families.

The National Committee to Free Ramsey Muñiz has been involved in seeking my husband's freedom for twenty-four years. His supporters believe in him for his heart and accomplishments. He contributed his talents for the sake of others.

Ramsey is now seventy-five years of age, and his health has greatly declined. In 2016, he had pneumonia, chronic obstructive pulmonary disease, and congestive heart failure. He has been near death several times, as complications of pneumonia continue to arise.

Ramsey's family, friends, and supporters will never abandon the efforts to obtain his freedom. He will always be loved by his family and by many others who know his heart. He has been imprisoned unjustly and unlawfully for twenty-four years.

For those who read this book, we ask that you pray for Ramsey Muñiz. His suffering has been long and hard, and it is unjust. We thank God that he remains alive after all the injustice he has faced and continues to face to this day.

Those who wish to help can ask their congressional representative to contact the Director of the Bureau of Prisons and urge him to grant the immediate freedom of Ramsey Muñiz. For information, go to www.freeramsey.com.

Those who are wise will shine like the brightness
of the heavens, and those who lead many to
righteousness, like the stars forever and ever.

—Daniel 12:3

Seeking Justice

CHAPTER 6

The Law Falls Silent

Dr. Alan Bean is the executive director of *Friends of Justice*. He is an intellectual and spiritual leader who advocates for the imprisoned, knowing the circumstances that bring about their incarceration. Through the organization *Friends of Justice*, Dr. Bean has spent years helping the wrongfully incarcerated, including Ramsey Muñiz.

Upon learning of Muñiz's predicament, he decided to become involved in his case. We can never adequately thank Dr. Bean, his wife, Nancy, and their family for the work that they do to help others. Their contribution to the case of Ramiro "Ramsey" Muñiz has been invaluable.

As executive director of *Friends of Justice*, Dr. Bean maintains a blog in which he states their mission as being one of defending the poor and the wrongfully incarcerated. Several years ago, he made an analysis of Muñiz's 1994 case. After having spent a great deal of time doing research, he posted his interpretation of the trial, which was based totally on the information contained in the trial transcript.

The Law Falls Silent: The Conviction of a
Latino Icon Raises Troubling Questions

The government targeted Ramsey Muñiz on the uncorroborated word of a major narcotic importer. Then, by withholding this information, they made it impossible for the sharpest defense attorney in Texas to challenge their case until it was too late.

By Alan Bean
Friends of Justice

In the eyes of the law, Ramiro "Ramsey" Muñiz is a convicted drug dealer who refuses to take responsibility for his actions.

In a federal trial in 1994, a Texas jury found Muñiz guilty of participating in a narcotics conspiracy. Because he had two prior convictions, federal law dictated a life sentence without possibility of parole.

A growing community of supporters is asking President Barack Obama to commute Ramsey's sentence on humanitarian grounds. Ramsey Muñiz is approaching his seventieth birthday, and after a serious fall, he can no longer walk without the assistance of a cane. What good is accomplished, they ask, by keeping such a man in federal custody?

Others believe Muñiz was targeted as part of a political vendetta. Twice in the early 1970s, Ramsey was a gubernatorial candidate on the La Raza Unida ticket. Following a college football career with the Baylor Bears, Muñiz graduated from the university's law school. Handsome, charismatic, and tireless, Ramsey's political campaigns galvanized the Latino community, especially in the Rio Grande Valley. According to some of his stalwart supporters, Ramsey's Anglo opponents used the war on drugs to humiliate a Latino icon.

So, who is Ramsey Muñiz?

Is he the civil rights leader who shook up Texas politics? This is how Ramsey is remembered by his old friends from the halcyon days of La Raza Unida.

Is he the well-connected legal professional with a passion for defending young marijuana defendants? This is how his colleagues in the legal community remember him.

Is he a mystic-in-chains whose suffering has drawn him into deep communion with the crucified Christ? This is the Ramsey who greets a steady stream of visitors at the Beaumont Medium prison.

Or is Muñiz just an unprincipled opportunist who used his professional standing as a front for get-rich-quick drug deals? This is how Muñiz was portrayed in a federal courtroom in 1994, and it is how he is still regarded in the eyes of the law.

When a man is driving a car with forty kilos of powdered cocaine in the trunk, he certainly looks guilty. But who put the drugs in the car, and did Ramsey know the drugs were there?

This wasn't the first time the hero of the Chicano movement was associated with the drug business. In 1976, Ramsey was accused of participating in a conspiracy to import marijuana into the United States. A young codefendant negotiated a dramatic sentence reduction by agreeing to name every person who had been present when the importation of marijuana was discussed. Ramsey Muñiz was one of the names.

Like most Latinos in South Texas, Muñiz regarded marijuana as the moral equivalent of beer or wine, a common feature of social life that posed no moral problems when used in moderation. But when the Nixon administration associated the prolific plant with hippies, Mexicans, and radical war protesters, the war on drugs was born.

Many former supporters were dismayed when Muñiz entered a guilty plea. He was a lawyer, not a drug dealer, so why was he going down without a fight?

Muñiz was uniquely vulnerable to federal narcotics conspiracy charges. Many of the leading marijuana importers in the Rio Grande Valley came from socially prominent families who had supported La Raza Unida in the early 1970s and regarded Ramsey Muñiz as a celebrity figure. According to federal law, a defendant can participate in a conspiracy without knowing all of his coconspirators and with only scant information about the nature of the conspiracy. You don't even have to profit personally. If you know illegal transactions are taking place and you fail to blow the whistle, you are part of the conspiracy.

Muñiz freely admits that he was privy to conversations related to marijuana importation. He thought he was protected from prosecution by attorney-client privilege. He was wrong.

Humiliated by his dramatic fall from grace, Muñiz wanted to disappear as quickly, quietly, and completely as possible. Two virtually identical cases had been filed on the basis of the same conspiracy allegations, one in San Antonio, the other in Corpus Christi. After taking a plea offer to avoid the humiliation of trial, Ramsey was sentenced to two consecutive five-year terms and shipped off to McNeil Island, a prison on the Washington State coast commonly reserved for gang members.

After serving half his term, Ramsey Muñiz returned to the free world and, having forfeited his law license, began a new career as a paralegal. His specialty was helping Anglo attorneys communicate with Latino clients. To his great surprise, his time in prison had given him instant credibility with drug defendants and their families. They assumed that a man who had done time would understand the fear and confusion they were feeling.

They were right. Ramsey knew too much about the routine horror of prison life to be blasé about the consequences of a narcotics conviction. Wherever he went, Muñiz was surrounded by the relatives of drug defendants desperate for effective legal assistance. If his clients had money, Ramsey hooked them up with a good attorney. But he frequently went to bat for indigent defendants as well, even when the cases he sponsored were sure to lose money for the law firms he represented. Attorneys shook their heads in bewilderment but often yielded to Ramsey's zealous advocacy.

Muñiz was in Dallas visiting with the families of marijuana defendants when he was arrested in March 1994. When he went to trial a few months later, the attorneys he once worked for painted a composite portrait of a morally driven crusader, a man determined to weave some justice out of his own suffering.

In the eighteen years since he was arrested in the parking lot of a La Quinta motel in Dallas, Ramsey's spiritual education has continued. His first teacher was Diego Duran, a sixteenth-century Spanish missionary, whose writings preserved much of what we know of traditional Mexican religion. Connecting with the religious roots of Mexico's indigenous people strengthened his commitment to the Roman Catholic piety of his childhood.

In 2009, Ramsey experienced the first of many vivid night visitations from significant people from his past. These visions lack the disconnected and logically bizarre quality of normal dreams. The conversation is natural, Ramsey says, "Just like you were sitting across from me and we were talking. I can reach out and touch my visitors, and they can touch me. In every respect, it is just like real life. Most nights, I have normal dreams or no dreams at all, but in the hours before a visitation, I can feel the Spirit growing inside me, and I know that tonight will be one of those nights."

The most frequent night visitor is Ramsey's father-in-law, Dr. Salvador Álvarez. "We were very close while he was still alive," Ramsey told me, "we were tight."

Ramsey's nocturnal encounters, especially with Álvarez, have been life-transforming. "Ramsey, do you love?" his father-in-law asked one night.

Confused, Ramsey said, "Yes, I love. Why do you ask?"

"When you speak of love," Álvarez replied, "it is always for your own people, la raza. Nuestra gente. Have you no love for the rest of the world?"

"I realized he was right," Ramsey says. "It isn't enough to love your own people; it is also necessary to love people who are not like you. That's why I now sign all my letters, 'Freedom, justice, and love for the entire world.'"

Muñiz would be an excellent candidate for a presidential commutation if he would express remorse for his crimes, and many wonder why he is so adamant on this point when, at first glance, the government's case against him seems airtight.

Consider the facts the government presented to the jury in the summer of 1994:

On the evening of March 10, 1994, agents with Drug Enforcement Administration in Dallas saw Muñiz pick up an unidentified man at the Love Field airport in Dallas, Texas.

The following morning, Muñiz had breakfast with an associate named Juan Gonzales and the unidentified man he met at the airport. In the course of conversation, the unidentified man referenced a deal scheduled for ten o'clock.

After breakfast, Muñiz and Gonzales dropped off the unidentified man at Love Field and returned to the Ramada Inn.

Muñiz got behind the wheel of a white Mercury Topaz and followed Gonzales to a La Quinta motel one mile south on Interstate 35.

When agents from the Dallas office of the Drug Enforcement Administration questioned Muñiz moments after he exited the Topaz, he concealed the keys and denied any association with the car.

The trunk was opened, revealing forty kilograms of powder cocaine with a street value of $800,000.

That's all the government wanted the jury to know about Ramsey Muñiz. It was then up to Dick DeGuerin, Ramsey's high-profile defense attorney, to muddy the waters as much as he could. A string of attorneys who had employed Ramsey as a legal assistant talked about his passion for helping indigent defendants. Testimony showed that Ramsey was in Dallas in March 1994 because several families were desperate for his assistance.

As civil rights attorney Michelle Alexander recently told Stephen Colbert, "During the 1990s, the period of the greatest escalation in the drug war, nearly 80 percent of the increase in drug arrests were for marijuana possession, saddling these young people with criminal records for life that will authorize legal discrimination against them in employment, housing, access to education, and public benefits."

Ramsey Muñiz was in Dallas, testimony suggested, trying to minimize the impact of the government's war on marijuana.

The jury also learned a little bit about the mystery man Muñiz picked up at the Dallas airport on Thursday night and deposited at the same airport Friday morning. Donacio Medina was a Mexican businessman who came to Texas seeking legal representation for two brothers, one in Texas, the other in California, who were awaiting trial on federal drug charges.

Testimony suggested that Donacio Medina was introduced to Ramsey Muñiz by Moises Andrade, a businessman who owned camera shops on both sides of the Texas-Mexico border. When Medina mentioned his brothers' legal troubles, Andrade directed him to Ramsey Muñiz.

Medina wanted his brothers sentenced to as little time as possible, and then, after they were sentenced, he was hoping to have them transferred to prisons in Mexico—a little-known feature of the recently adopted NAFTA agreement made this kind of prisoner swap possible. Well-connected and fully bilingual, Muñiz was the ideal person to help Medina negotiate with a high-profile Texas attorney.

Finally, defense counsel used motel phone logs to prove that virtually every call Ramsey made while in Dallas was either to his wife or a long list of prospective clients. The implication was that Muñiz came to North Texas on a legitimate business trip; doing a drug deal with a virtual stranger wasn't on the agenda.

The jury also learned that Muñiz drove from Houston to Dallas in a red Toyota Camry driven by Juan Gonzales, a laborer from the Rio Grande Valley who frequently served as Ramsey's chauffeur. Muñiz explained that he got more work done when he paid someone else to do the driving. Due to a medical emergency, Gonzales made a hurried dash to his home in South Texas, and for most of his time in the Dallas area, Muñiz was picked up and dropped off by potential clients.

Finally, the jury was told that the white Topaz Muñiz was driving just prior to his arrest had been rented in Houston by Donacio Medina, using Juan Gonzales's Sears credit card. Gonzales told Medina that he couldn't use his card because his account was $300 in arrears, so Medina paid off the balance with cash so Gonzales could rent the car. This happened short days before Muñiz and Gonzales drove to Dallas.

Dick DeGuerin did some sleuthing while the trial was underway, and the results were stunning. Prior to trial, the prosecution had portrayed the Muñiz prosecution as an in-house job. DEA agents in Dallas got a call from suspicious employees of the Ramada Inn, put Muñiz and Gonzales under surveillance, and the rest is history.

But when DeGuerin ran the official scenario past motel personnel, he sparked a chorus of denials. No one associated with the Ramada Inn thought their courteous and professionally dressed guests were the least bit suspicious, and no one had called the DEA office in Dallas. The government's story was a complete fabrication.

There was more. Phone records showed that on March 9, Donacio Medina called Ramsey Muñiz from the Classic Inn, a low-end motel in Fort Worth. This meant that Medina had traveled to Fort Worth prior to March 9, 1994; returned to Houston on March 9; and flew back to Dallas the following day. This meant that Medina was in Houston on parts of March 9, 10, and 11 (the day Muñiz was arrested).

The weird revelations kept coming. On the last day of trial, DeGuerin got a DEA agent to admit that Danny Hernandez, a criminal informant working with the DEA, had booked into Fort Worth's Classic Inn on March 6 and maintained a room at the motel during all of Medina's shuttle diplomacy between Houston and Dallas. The DEA agent insisted that Hernandez was working a completely different case. The agent insisted that Hernandez had no association with Medina and that no records suggested that Medina had ever stayed at the Classic Inn. But if that was true, why did Medina call Muñiz from the Classic Inn on March 9, and why, as trial testimony suggests, did Medina pay Danny Gallardo, an off-duty FedEx driver, to transport him to the Classic Inn shortly after arriving at Love Field the following day? Furthermore, why did the mysterious Danny Hernandez book into the Fort Worth motel claiming that he had no identification because his wallet had been stolen? If that was true, where did Hernandez get the money for the room, and why did he give the motel a fake address? Did Medina and Hernandez drive to Fort Worth in the white Topaz Medina rented with Juan Gonzales's Sears card so that Medina could enjoy a base of operations without leaving a paper trail?

The final revelation arrived just as Dick DeGuerin was putting the finishing touches on his closing argument. Newly revealed government records showed that Donacio Medina had been "negotiating" with the DEA office in Houston. DeGuerin referenced this fact during his close, but with no time to think through all the implications, he didn't know what to do with the information. It is likely that the prosecution revealed this information to the defense as soon as they learned about it. If so, both the prosecution and the defense went to trial knowing next to nothing about the man at the heart of the story.

What does this shocking piece of information imply?

First, it meant that the Muñiz operation originated in Houston and that DEA agents in Dallas joined the investigation late and only at the request of the Houston office.

Second, it means that, shortly after arriving in Houston from Mexico, Medina was arrested and "debriefed" by the DEA. What probable cause did the Houston DEA have for picking up Donacio Medina?

We can only speculate. Shortly after being convicted, Muñiz learned through the prison grapevine that an undercover DEA agent overheard Medina bragging about the size of his cocaine operation at a Houston party. Obviously, this theory can't be documented.

It is also possible that Medina was picked up because two of his brothers were sitting in federal prisons awaiting trial on charges involving enormous amounts of powdered cocaine. One brother was found with almost $5 million in his possession. Two brothers facing narcotics charges suggested that Donacio had a stake in the family business.

Here's what can be said for certain: Medina agreed to help the feds build a narcotics case against Ramsey Muñiz in exchange for free passage back to Mexico. Trial testimony shows that Medina was held at Love Field by DEA agents until forty kilos of powdered cocaine were discovered in the trunk of the white Topaz. The moment the drugs were discovered, Medina was released.

Was the federal government targeting Ramsey Muñiz? This question cannot be answered with certainty. Ramsey's name may have come up when the DEA asked Medina what he was doing in the country. If Medina claimed to be in Houston looking for legal representation for his brothers, Ramsey's name would have dropped and a quick check would have revealed his prior narcotics conviction.

This would have suggested that, his cover story notwithstanding, Medina had entered the country to do a narcotics deal with an underworld figure named Ramsey Muñiz. It is possible that the DEA officials who targeted Muñiz knew nothing of his political history.

Confronted with the government's suspicions, Medina faced a simple choice: deny that he and Muñiz had a drug deal in the mix and join his brothers in a federal prison awaiting trial or give the feds Muñiz in exchange for a one-way ticket to Mexico City.

It is possible, of course, that the Houston DEA got it right. The fact that Muñiz drove a narcotics-laden car down a one-mile stretch of I-35 is entirely consistent with the government's theory. The prosecution had no burden to show who placed the drugs in the Topaz or who the prospective buyers might have been. Prior to trial, the government wasn't even required to inform defense counsel of their relationship to Donacio Medina or any other criminal informant. In fact, the prosecution likely went to trial knowing very little (and caring even less) about Medina's association to the Houston DEA.

With the striking exception of a single country, testimony from criminal informants is viewed with grave suspicion in the free world, and for obvious reasons. Alexandra Natapoff is America's foremost authority on the use and abuse of "snitch" testimony.

"Criminal informants are an important piece of the wrongful conviction puzzle," she says, "because *informants have such predictable and powerful inducements to lie*, because law enforcement relies heavily on their information, and because the system is not well designed to check that information."

There are two enormous problems with the government's case against Ramsey Muñiz (and virtually every other federal case built on snitch testimony). First, the government targeted Muñiz on the uncorroborated word of a man they believed to be a major narcotics importer. Second, by withholding this information, the government made it impossible for the sharpest defense attorney in Texas to challenge the government's theory of the crime.

Did Ramsey Muñiz know he was transporting narcotics? That's the only question that matters. The government shaped the evidence to make it appear that he did, while making it impossible for defense counsel to argue that he didn't. In a nutshell, that's what's wrong with this case.

The government argued that Muñiz got behind the wheel of the white Topaz because it was his prearranged role in a narcotics conspiracy. That's a nice, simple story, and deprived of an alternative explanation, the jury was sure to buy it. But there are plenty of alternative explanations.

Consider this scenario. Confronted with DEA suspicions, Medina "confesses" that he came to Texas to do a drug deal with Ramsey Muñiz. Knowing that Juan Gonzales would soon be driving Muñiz to Dallas, Medina rents a car for two days in Gonzales's name, and Gonzales goes along with the plan because it restores his credit and places $250 of free money in his pocket.

Next, the DEA gives Medina and Danny Hernandez forty

kilos of cocaine. The two men place the drugs in the trunk of the rented Mercury Topaz and drive to the Classic Inn in Fort Worth. Hernandez rents a room without identification so there will be no record of Medina's stay.

Medina flies back to Houston at the request of the DEA (while Hernandez guards the stash); then Medina arranges to have Ramsey Muñiz pick him up at Love Field on the evening of March 10 so the Dallas DEA can witness the two men together.

The next step can be reconstructed from trial testimony. Medina approaches Danny Gallardo, an off-duty FedEx driver, and asks him to drive to the Classic Inn in Fort Worth on the evening of March 10 so Medina can pick up his car. After arriving at the motel, Medina tells Gallardo that the car isn't there and asks to be driven to the Ramada Inn in Lewisville. Seeing Muñiz in the Ramada parking lot, Medina exits the car and Gallardo drives off. Medina then gets into a car driven by an unidentified man and disappears until the following morning.

Trial testimony suggests that, on the morning of March 11, Ramsey Muñiz, Donacio Medina, and Juan Gonzales (recently returned from a whirlwind trip to the Rio Grande Valley) meet for breakfast at the Owens restaurant across the street from the motel. At some point, Medina slips Gonzales the keys to the rented white Topaz and asks him to return the vehicle for him.

The three men drive to Love Field shortly before eleven o'clock on the morning of March 11. Medina gets out of the car and disappears inside the terminal. According to trial testimony, Gonzales stops en route to the Ramada Inn to call a relative from a pay phone. Only then does Gonzales inform Muñiz that he plans to spend the night at the La Quinta that evening and ask his boss to help him move Medina's rented car from the Ramada to the La Quinta. Although Ramsey doesn't have a driver's license, he agrees to make the one-mile trip as a favor to Gonzales. Trial testimony suggests that Gonzales, learning that Muñiz intended to fly back to Houston after a noon meeting with prospective clients, decided to remain in the DFW area to look for work. The details remain sketchy, however, because Gonzales didn't discuss his plans with Muñiz prior to arrest and because Gonzales didn't testify at trial.

Was Ramsey Muñiz innocently moving a car for a friend, or was he engaged in an illegal narcotics deal? The answer depends on whether you believe Donacio Medina or Ramsey Muñiz.

This recreation of the story involves considerable speculation, but so does the government's theory of the crime. Both reconstructions may be wildly off base. The real story may be buried somewhere in an obscure DEA file folder, but given the slim corpus of facts at our disposal, partisans on either side of the story are reduced to playing a guessing game.

Several questions may never be answered. Did Medina supply the drugs in the trunk of the Topaz, or did the forty kilos of cocaine come from a DEA evidence locker? Both theories are possible.

The more you know about this case, the more troubling it becomes. Let's begin with Donacio Medina. If DEA suspicions are justified (and I suspect they are), we are dealing with a man with an established narcotics distribution network trained and equipped to do his dirty business for him. Why would such a man travel to Texas to do a drug deal with Ramsey Muñiz when he could do this kind of transaction from the safety of his armchair?

And if Medina came to Texas to do a narcotics transaction with Muñiz, why didn't the deal go down in Houston or in the Rio Grande Valley, where illegal narcotics are cheaper and more readily available? Why jump through all the logistical hoops a Dallas deal demanded? The most likely scenario is that Medina flew to Dallas because that's where Muñiz was doing business. But if Ramsey had a million-dollar drug deal in the works, why was he spending so much time with pissant marijuana defendants?

Here's the simplest explanation: Medina planted the drugs in the Topaz and, working through Gonzales, placed Muñiz behind the wheel because that's what his deal with the Houston DEA demanded.

Is an innocent and deeply spiritual man living behind bars

because a Mexican drug lord was desperate to save his own skin? Of all the theories on the table, this one makes the most sense.

So why doesn't the Department of Justice release Ramsey Muñiz because, innocent or not, he has paid his debt to society?

Two reasons. First, Ramsey's innocence, however likely, cannot be proven. Since there is no parole in the federal legal system, the life sentence stands.

Second, the government can't back away from the Muñiz fiasco without admitting that America's war on drugs has thoroughly corrupted the federal justice system. Cases based on the uncorroborated testimony of drug dealers are guaranteed to convict the innocent along with the guilty. A morally flawed criminal with a gun to his head will say whatever the triggerman wants him to say.

Snitch testimony is inherently unreliable; that's why the United States is the only nation in the free world that builds criminal cases on such a flimsy foundation. Unfortunately, America's war on drugs cannot be waged without criminal informants.

Without the drug war, we are told, all hell would break loose. If a few thousand innocent Americans get locked up in the process, that's just the price we have to pay. The Roman orator Cicero summed it up nicely a century before Jesus was crucified: "In time of war, the law falls silent."

It is appropriate that Ramsey Muñiz identifies so closely with the suffering of Christ crucified. Like his Savior, Ramsey has been sacrificed for the greater good. "You do not understand," Caiaphas told the religious leaders of his day, "that it is better for you to have one man die for the people than to have the whole nation destroyed."

This perverse but powerful logic keeps men like Ramsey Muñiz in bondage. If he would only admit guilt and feign contrition, Muñiz might have been released long ago. But like he says, "How do you express remorse for something you didn't do?" If you are willing to abandon your last shred of self-respect, it's easy. But men like Ramsey Muñiz can't walk through that door.

There is only one way to resolve this dilemma. Barack Obama could issue a presidential commutation on humanitarian grounds. But the president can't make this bold move unless we move first. Abraham Lincoln got it right: "With public sentiment, nothing can fail; without it, nothing can succeed. Consequently, he who molds public sentiment goes deeper than he who enacts statutes or pronounces decisions. He makes statutes and decisions possible or impossible to be executed."

What Franklin Roosevelt told a group of Depression-era reformers, Barack Obama says to us, "I agree with you, I want to do it ... now make me do it."

After letters of support from congressmen, resolutions passed by national organizations, hundreds of letters from supporters, petitions with thousands of signatures, and letters petitioning foreign dignitaries, one can only ask what it takes for a president to make the right decision on a case based on its own merits. Perhaps such a decision should be made by people from all walks of life, including those who understand the suffering that comes from imprisonment.

Blessed are those who are persecuted because of righteousness, for theirs is the kingdom of heaven.

—Matthew 5:10

CHAPTER 7

Dreams of Heaven

I devoted years of study at Harvard Divinity School and received a doctorate of theology. Throughout the years, I spent time researching scripture, growing in faith and intelligence, and devoting time to prayer. This involved years of dedication, yet those years did not prepare me to comprehend the blessings given to Muñiz because of his suffering. Among these blessings are dreams of heaven, which are not ordinary dreams. He is blessed with the presence of his loving mother, father, grandmother, brother, mother-in-law, and father-in-law. There are others, but these are the central figures who communicate with him. The one thing that they have in common is their love for him. They are also all deceased.

An interesting phenomenon takes place when he has these dreams. It is difficult to wake him up. When speaking to his wife by phone, Muñiz has shared that at times others have tried to wake him. Often, this takes time. They call out to him and shake his body, but he does not stir. It is as if he is in a trance as he sleeps.

I cannot explain the experiences that Muñiz has through his dreams. Loved ones speak to him and convey profound insight. He is told that he is given these dreams because of his suffering, faith, and love for God. Although he devotes his prayers to God,

Jesus Christ, and La Virgen de Guadalupe, he also asks for loved ones to come into his heart. Their presence, made possible through God, gives him the greatest gift anyone could receive—words from heaven. As he sleeps, loved ones make their presence known in his world (or he in theirs). He has many questions, yet he often refrains from speaking, knowing that there is a great deal that others have to convey.

Muñiz is humbled by the spiritual dreams that he has, for he knows what they represent. To him, they are holy encounters. He calls out to those he loves, knowing that they will speak to him, pray for him, and pray to God with him. At times, they embrace him. Such encounters are so unfamiliar that sometimes he wakes up panting, realizing what has taken place and wondering where he is.

Loving family members visit Muñiz and make their presence known regularly and during times of sadness and sorrow. The experience is so overwhelming that his mattress becomes soaked with tears—but not tears of sorrow. He cries from a sense of gratitude, having received such love from an encounter that is unfamiliar. The experience transforms Muñiz into a new person filled with life that is instilled by love from heaven.

The spiritual messages conveyed to Muñiz are profound. He has no other way to explain vocabulary he does not use, concepts described in different ways, and answers to questions that cannot be proven by man. The information leads me to believe that his encounters are celestial.

There is no doubt in Muñiz's mind that he communicates with loving family members and others. At first, his recollections are vague, but with time, details begin to surface in his mind. One of the earlier dreams he has shared pertained to the dreams themselves. Muñiz recalled the following words: "Cuida a tus sueños. Cuidalos porque no son tuyos. Dios le los ha prestado y un día, cuando te vayas de este mundo, tendrás que regresarlos." These words are translated into English as "Take care of your dreams. Take care of them because these they are not yours. God has loaned them to you, and one day, when you depart from this world, you will need to return them" (Muñiz dream, 2010).

Many of the dreams that Muñiz has are of his mother, Hilda. Her messages contain the love and pride that she has for her son because of his character, strength, and love. She appears to her son when his suffering is great and when he is ill and alone. Her words of pride and encouragement bring recollections of the loving person that he was as a child and the beautiful soul that he has possessed throughout his life. She gives a loving and healing embrace that can only come from a mother. Muñiz recalls the loving words in one of his encounters with his mother: "From the time and day that I have known, my son, you were always concerned about others and never about yourself. That is the reason that God shall forever be with you and with Irma" (Muñiz dream of Hilda Longoria Muñiz, August 23, 2012).

The late Dr. Salvador Álvarez was Muñiz's father-in-law. There was mutual love and respect between them. Dr. Álvarez is remembered for being a spiritual man who had great love and devotion to God and his family. He was an educated man whose conversations were often profound and philosophical.

Dr. Álvarez has been a principal figure in Muñiz's dreams. He has conveyed words of wisdom, many of which pertain to the ways of God. The messages that Dr. Álvarez has conveyed provide insight with great clarity. They give Muñiz purpose and hope during sorrowful times as he states,

> Ramsey, my son, historically, even if you were poor and lowly, even if your mother and father were the poorest of the poor, your lineage was not considered. Only your way of life mattered. The purity of your heart and soul. Your good and pure humane heart. Your present loving, stout heart. It is said in heaven that you have God in your heart and that you are wise and love in the things of God (Muñiz dream of Dr. Salvador Álvarez, July 26, 2014).

Ramsey, to know that God knows all things is true peace. All faith and all trust in God are true wisdom and intelligence. To understand how God loves us is to understand how we are to love one another. That is true love, and it brings us true peace and tranquility amid the turmoil and strife that is constantly within the lives on earth. Looking for control without God is like surviving in the desert without water. It cannot be done. Remember, Ramsey, with God even the impossible is possible, and you are so right when you pray to God. Spirituality is the key to any movement pertaining to freedom, justice, and love (Muñiz dream of Dr. Salvador Álvarez, November 7, 2011).

Ramsey, spiritual paradise is hidden in each one of us. It is concealed within you too, right now. If you wish, it will come for you in reality, tomorrow even, and for the rest of your life. Indeed, it is true that when humanity understands this thought, the kingdom of heaven will come to them no longer in a dream, but in reality (Muñiz dream of Dr. Salvador Álvarez, October 28, 2013).

Ramsey, becoming aware of your true being creates a resonating field of miracles that can get stronger and stronger without end. This is because you're entering into a flow of something bigger than your individuality. It's the power of God's earth waking up to heal itself after being asleep for so many generations, and you are the key and the symbol of freedom, justice, and love like never before (Muñiz dream of Dr. Salvador Álvarez, 2013).

Muñiz is taken aback by his spiritual encounters, and he is humbled to receive such a blessing. His dreams provide love and consolation through messages that are given to him from heaven. He has shared the following words with his wife, Irma, describing a dream when he was extremely ill:

> I was embraced by my mother, Hilda; your mom; and Grandmother Rosa like never before spiritually, and we all prayed together. I woke up this morning feeling like as if I was just born all over again—no cold, no running nose, no headache, no body aches, and feeling as if I was ready to play four quarters of football. This is the power of God's spirituality and love (Muñiz dream, August 7, 2015).

At times, I have wondered why Muñiz would receive such profound dreams and communications. One might argue that his mind is protecting him from the horror of prison life. I believe that his encounters are real, and in a dream, Dr. Salvador Álvarez conveys that Muñiz receives God's blessings because of his uncompromising faith and love:

> Ramsey, my son, know in your heart and soul that Jesus Christ loves you dearly for the spiritual man that you are regardless of the imprisonment, chains, shackles, and hunger. You have gotten on your knees to thank God Almighty for your life, strength, courage, valor, spirituality, and most of all love. In your heart and soul, you know that God is love and love is God (Muñiz dream, 2016).

An interesting thing to mention about the dreams is that they often refer to suffering and the fight for freedom. In messages conveyed by Dr. Álvarez, Muñiz gains strength from his inspiration and encouragement, which carries him throughout the day.

Ramsey, my son, don't ever stop fighting for your freedom. Spiritually, God is freedom, and we must forever seek our freedom as we seek the presence of God in our lives, in our families, in humanity, and most importantly in our hearts and souls (Muñiz dream of Dr. Salvador Álvarez March 30, 2016).

In November 2016, Muñiz became ill with a severe case of aspiration pneumonia, a life-threatening illness for which he was medically treated several times. Because of the infection, his health declined, and he lost the ability to swallow correctly, making doctors and others believe he would not survive. He battled congestive heart failure, chronic obstructive pulmonary disease, kidney disease, and an irregular heartbeat. One doctor stated that he demonstrated signs of having suffered a stroke. In his weakened state, Muñiz had dreams of loved ones in the spirit world, who encouraged him to live. Muñiz recalls the words of his mother, Hilda: "Levantate, Mijo. Te tienes que levantar. Enseñales quien eres y la sangre que corre en tus venas. Enseñales el hombre que yo traje a este mundo. Eres el hijo que Dios me pidió." Translated into English, the words are "Get up, Son. You must get up. Show them who you are, the blood that runs in your veins, and the man that I brought into this world. You are the son that God asked of me" (Muñiz dream of Hilda Longoria Muñiz, June 30, 2017).

Rosario Longoria Campos, Muñiz's grandmother, provided love and encouragement to him, making her presence known throughout his illness. She came to him in a dream, reminding him not to forget to drink hot tea. The following morning, Muñiz used a spoon to take small sips of hot tea. Shortly after, he began to cough and expel great amounts of phlegm.

Muñiz had a special relationship with his grandmother. He kept her at home and remained close to her during the last years of her life. He held her when she passed, so it is easy to understand how Rosario Longoria Campos would express her love to him in a dream: "Eras un niño, y cresiste a ser un muchacho jovencito.

Ahora eres el hombre que Dios nos pidió en este mundo. Desde que eras niño, supimos que fuiste un regalo de Dios para nosotros." In English, the words are translated as "You were a child and grew to be a young boy. Now you are the man that God asked of us in this world. Since you were a child, we knew that you were a gift to us from God" (Muñiz dream of Rosario Longoria Campus 2015).

The most beautiful words shared by Muñiz describe the manner in which he prays. He prays for the spirits who communicate with him, for his family members on earth, and for many others whose names he calls out one at a time.

There is none closer to Muñiz's heart than his mother, Hilda. His prayers for her are poignant, demonstrating the eternal love that exists between those in heaven and on earth. As he prays for his mother, he also calls out and unites with her once again: "Aquí estoy, Mamacita. Aquí estoy. Yo soy el hombre que tu trajiste a este mundo. Dame tu misma fuerza, tu mismo amor, y tu orgullo de ser tuyo, Mamá. Aquí estoy. Estoy para servirte a ti, a Dios, Jesús Cristo, La Virgen de Guadalupe, y a todos nuestros espiritus que están en el cielo." His words translated into English are "I am here, Mother. I am here. I am the one that you brought into this world. Give me your strength, your love, and the pride that you taught me in being your son. I am here. I am here to serve you, God, Jesus Christ, Our Lady of Guadalupe, and all of the holy spirits who are in heaven" (Muñiz dream, 2017).

There have been many messages given to Muñiz through dreams from heaven. Those messages are significant in that they represent the most important things in life, which include love for God and the love of family.

During the darkest moments of his life, family members have remained with Muñiz because of the love that exists between them. This eternal love is the greatest gift given to us, enabling us to help each other and maintain unity in heaven and on earth.

I have asked Muñiz what his dreams represent. He shared,

It indicates that God knows of my pain, suffering, and everything that I have had to endure unfairly and oppressively, with such negative attitudes against my life. God knows that this had to be known to the entire world.

I know that I was spiritually chosen to be someone. Even my grandmother Rosa would say, "Tu eres muy especial. Fuiste mandado por Dios." I came to understand and believe this, knowing that I was the first in elementary school, junior high school, and in high school.

When I suffered illness and was near death, I heard the doctors say that they did not know how I was able to live. I remember that in my weakest condition I turned to them and said, "God wishes for me to live, and I still have some things to do for Him" (Personal communication, 2017).

May the groans of the prisoners come before you;
with your strong arm preserve those condemned to die.

—Psalm 79:11

Faith in the Midst of Suffering

CHAPTER 8

Suffering

I ask myself how people maintain their faith in times of suffering. Many who suffer lose their faith, believing that they have been abandoned by God. As we progress through life, however, we realize that all people suffer. Jesus Christ was the son of God, and he had to experience the greatest forms of suffering in order to save the world.

Muñiz shares his views on suffering, pointing out that suffering, which defines who we are, has been in existence from the beginning of time. God shows suffering many ways, so that we can understand the extent of the suffering that exists in the world.

People deal with suffering in different ways. Many resent their suffering while others embrace it for the rest of their lives. There are also those who take pleasure in the suffering of others and even wish it upon them. True strength and power, however, are found when we seek God's presence in times of suffering.

Knowing the difficulty of dealing with suffering, we can only wonder about the impact that faith has in times of sorrow. In the words of Muñiz, "To believe in God is to be free. Many people have not experienced or lived this pureness or have been sensitive to the presence of God in their lives. Some have never even known love.

Sometimes this is not their fault, and sometimes it is. Only God can make this determination."

Through Muñiz, I have come to believe that God is with us, especially in times of suffering. Those who maintain their faith will come to understand this. After all that he has experienced because of his suffering, Muñiz shares, "Once you believe, the heavens will open up before you. God will open your heart, your mind, and things of heaven will come to you."

Many people find suffering difficult to accept. Some ask about the presence of God in times of sorrow. Even Muñiz questioned the purpose of suffering and was told that when people suffer and when they die, they give life to others. He recalled a dream in which Dr. Álvarez stated, "We know that you complain of the suffering you have experienced and the manner in which it is felt. God gave you life as a result, so that you could give life to others who would learn that in suffering there can be love, spirituality, and the presence of God. Your suffering gives life to others because of what it represents spiritually" (Muñiz dream of Dr. Salvador Álvarez, 2017).

Recently Muñiz has spoken about his suffering. He has been chained, shackled, hungry, lonely, and cold in the dark. He has also faced serious illness. Muñiz has been near death and unable to breathe to the point of being unresponsive. His suffering and sadness have been immense, yet he has maintained faith and love. He now understands through his experiences about heaven that suffering increases the spiritual awareness in others, and brings them closer to God. Knowing that suffering impacts people's lives, Muñiz offers his suffering for others, and prays for them individually.

Muñiz receives encouragement from deceased family members through dreams which pertain to his suffering. This has helped him cope with the suffering and sadness he has endured. Dr. Álvarez has told him, "Ramsey, your heaven is found in solidarity with those who seek freedom, justice, and love for all humanity. For today you are presently suffering a hell consumed by earthly injustice against your soul. Because of your drastic suffering and oppressive imprisonment, you have given freedom, justice, and love a face for those who seek the same on earth and in heaven" (Muñiz dream of Dr. Salvador Álvarez, 2011). In a letter to his wife Muñiz states, "In my conversation, your father shared that one must suffer and feel the pain of humanity in order to be chosen by God and Jesus Christ. He stated that many who are at the right hand of God and Jesus Christ have not suffered, but at one time or another they gave their lives in sacrifice, fulfilling the needs and teachings of Jesus Christ. The most powerful and human gift to extend involves suffering with pain, with agony, with oppression and imprisonment. That is when God seeks his or her heart and soul. When that person tries to bring freedom, justice, and love to all humanity, he or she is doing what God seeks to give to the world" (Personal letter from Muñiz to his wife, 2011).

The most profound insight given to Muñiz pertains to suffering. It was five years ago that his father-in-law, Dr. Salvador Álvarez, shared the following words in a dream: "Ramsey, we know that you have suffered drastically and with such pain and agony of the soul. The family has suffered just as much as you, but they continue to be strong spiritually with a lot of faith in their hearts and souls. The day will come soon that you will be free once again, for you must always remember that human freedom is a gift from God that serves as an example of His infinite divine goodness for justice and love for all humanity."

> Ramsey, why is God's entry into your human life and soul such good news? Well, for one thing, it means that the God of the universe really understands what it's like to be human, and to be like you and I. When we struggle with the challenges and disappointments of human life, we can be assured that God understands from the inside. But more importantly, the fact that God became human in Jesus Christ means that in the end God dealt with

our fundamental human problems of sin, jealousy, envy, and the lack of love in the hearts and souls of humanity. Because Jesus was both fully God and fully human, his death on the cross truly affected our salvation. It is the same cross, Ramsey, that you have carried for twenty-three years of your confined spiritual life. The incarnation alone didn't do it. But the incarnation made possible the saving power of the crucifixion and resurrection. Because of Christmas, there will be Good Friday, and because of Good Friday, there will be Easter. This isn't just a nice creative story made up by some early Christian. It's the true story of what God has actually done for the family, for your freedom, for love, and for your salvation (Muñiz dream of Dr. Salvador Álvarez, 2016).

Although encouragement is the central theme in Muñiz's dreams, loving family members also express sorrow for his suffering. During a visit with his wife, Muñiz described a profound dream of the mothers in his life saying, "I told them that I was ready to go. I had suffered long enough. It was not necessary for me to continue to suffer." The reply was, "You have never been alone. We are with you. You are the example of how to live and believe in God. He has always been with you, and He has seen how you suffered for years in the most horrible conditions in chains, shackles, isolation, loneliness, cold, at times without clothing, because you are a prisoner." My mother, Hilda, stated, "They took everything except your mind and heart. You resisted to the point of pulling the chains off your heart and mind, but they are yours and cannot be taken. If they try, they will answer to God, Jesus Christ, and La Virgen de Guadalupe, and they better hope they will not have to face me" (Muñiz dream of Hilda Longoria Muñiz, 2018). During his dreams, several observed Muñiz realizing that he was totally asleep, yet crying and extending his arms in the air.

Those who question the existence of God should take comfort in knowing that He is with the imprisoned and with the sick. He is with the lonely and with those who are dying. God loves those who suffer for His sake, and there is a spiritual purpose in suffering as Muñiz has been told by Dr. Salvador Álvarez: "Ramsey, always remember that there cannot be progress, freedom, or peace without a struggle and suffering" (Muñiz dream of Dr. Salvador Álvarez, July 22, 2012).

We all seek meaning in our suffering and we search for God in our lives. Although it seems that God does not hear us, He remains close to those who suffer because there is a purpose in suffering. It prevents others from suffering in the same way. This message has been given to Muñiz during the hardest times of his life.

In his dreams, Muñiz has been told that he is a symbol of love, spirituality, courage, strength, and freedom. Setting this example is important to God, who knows that the world is in great need of it. Muñiz is blessed for demonstrating that love, spirituality, courage, strength, freedom, and faith can exist in the hardest circumstances. He states, "When one has no faith, he does not have Christ in his heart. When one does not have Christ, he has nothing" (Muñiz dream of Dr. Salvador Álvarez, 2017).

Through Muñiz, I have learned that God's presence is with those who suffer. His heart resides in prisons, hospitals, nursing homes, and places where there is suffering, sadness, and sorrow. We must never lose faith, hope, and love for God despite our suffering. When we embrace this faith, we open our minds to the potential for miraculous change. Answers come in ways that we do not expect, but we believe that they fulfill God's loving purpose for the human race. He demonstrated this through His son, Jesus Christ, who had to experience the greatest forms of suffering which would result in death. In doing so, he provided the means of giving freedom, justice, and love to all.

He has shown you, O mortal, what is good.
And what does the Lord require of you?
To act justly and to love mercy
and to walk humbly with your God.

—Micah 6:8

Protesters in Washington, DC

CHAPTER 9

The Struggle Continues

Muñiz remains unjustly imprisoned. The *National Committee to Free Ramsey Muñiz* has struggled for twenty-four years to obtain his freedom, and it is apparent to many people throughout the country that his imprisonment is political.

All post-conviction appeals filed *pro se* by Muñiz were denied. They were filed while he was in solitary confinement at the USP in Leavenworth, Kansas. His applications for commutation of sentence were also denied. The last two applications were denied during President Barack Obama's terms as president, leaving many people shocked and disappointed, questioning the moral character of all leaders.

Although the skillful actions of government agents may be deemed legal, in Muñiz's case, they were immoral and wrong. They led to the arrest, conviction, and unjust incarceration of an innocent man who was sentenced to life without parole. What makes this even more deplorable is that Muñiz is not a criminal. He is a good man with a kind heart who did so much to help many others.

The Criminal Complaint used to arrest Muñiz contained false information. If it were not for the trial witnesses who were finally brought to testify, this would never have been discovered. Other questions about this case might have been addressed. However, a gag order was put in place before the trial began.

The prosecution withheld information that would have disclosed the name of the culprit until it was too late. It was shown briefly at the end of the trial, and the jury was then asked to deliberate. Such tactics used in court proceedings are unacceptable, yet these are the types of court proceedings that Muñiz and others have faced.

The arrests, convictions, trials, and sentencing of Ramsey Muñiz represent the most unfair and unjust actions committed against a person's life. It is everyone's responsibility to make this right. There comes a time when we will all justify our actions after we depart from this world. We are all held accountable for the decisions we make in our lives.

Family members, congressmen, organizations, religious leaders, and supporters throughout the country have sent letters to various government representatives, disclosing this injustice and asking for their help. Some have responded, but many have remained silent. We need their help, and we ask congressmen to correct this grave injustice.

Ramiro Muñiz submitted an application for compassionate release in 2013, knowing that he met the criteria based on his age and chronic medical conditions, which could not have been foreseen at the time of sentencing. The application was approved by his unit team and warden in 2016, and a probation officer was sent to his home to determine that he would have a place and someone to care for him. The application was forwarded to Washington, DC. More than five months passed, and he received no communication about his application. Everything came to a halt.

After he had received medical care for a debilitating illness, those in Washington, DC, asked for an updated medical evaluation. They determined that Muniz's condition had improved and that he no longer qualified for a reduction in sentence. His application was denied. Since then he became gravely ill, and remains fighting for his life.

Muniz has faced health issues since his early years of

incarceration. As he was undergoing emergency gallbladder surgery, his bile duct was nicked, and he spent time fighting infection in his body. He suffered chronic degenerative hip damage from a fall in Leavenworth, Kansas. Since December 2016, Muñiz has endured three separate hospitalizations for aspiration pneumonia, chronic obstructive pulmonary disease (COPD), congestive heart failure, atrial fibrillation, and hypoxia. In November 2017, he came back after suffering acute respiratory failure, requiring mechanical ventilation. "Ramsey Muñiz's life is one of sheer grit and determination" (Abernethy 1966).

How is it that after such debilitative and life-threatening illness his petition for compassionate release was denied? The American justice system is an imperfect one. It has incarcerated men and women using overly harsh guidelines, and petitions for clemency are kept confidential. Nobody is entitled to know how the authorities arrive at their decisions.

The experience of helping an incarcerated loved one has made me realize why people express sadness and anger about the ineffectiveness of an unchanged justice system. Everyone agrees that the system is flawed, yet little has been done to correct it. This reflects a lack of regard for human life while the incarcerated perish in an isolated world of sadness and suffering. I pray for them, knowing how life-altering situations place them in an environment of oppression, sadness, loneliness, illness, neglect, and ongoing suffering. No prisoner is immune from this environment, and Muñiz has experienced it all.

Many people who are incarcerated seek mercy and forgiveness which for the most part is unattainable. Doesn't suffering deserve any kind of mercy? I often ask why people in the free world deserve forgiveness while the incarcerated do not. The incarcerated include people who are good, and those in the outside world include many who are bad. All people have a right to seek mercy and forgiveness. More importantly, they should have a fair chance of obtaining it when they meet the criteria for presidential pardons, commutations, and compassionate release.

A shift toward a more compassionate society is not solely the responsibility of government. It is the responsibility of God's families throughout the world. When the moral consciousness of humanity changes, a change in government will follow.

We appeal to Democrats, Republicans, Independents, and people of conscience to keep the case of Ramsey Muñiz alive with our united voices. The time has come to free Ramsey Muñiz. He has suffered long enough!

Historically, there has never been a greater need for change than now. The world has gone wrong, and it is time to restore it. We seek the assistance of those who feel destined to replace hatred and violence with love and compassion. We will do so through prayers and supplications to God, asking Him to free Ramsey Muñiz and others, and restore the human race, giving freedom, justice, spirituality, and love to all.

For more information, contact the *National Committee to Free Ramsey Muñiz.*

ENDNOTES

1. The Raza Unida Party was the first political party of the Chicanos in the United States. It started in Crystal City, Texas, on July 21, 1971.
2. LULAC started on February 17, 1929, mostly by War World I veterans who fought to end racial and ethnic discrimination against Latinos and Latinas in the United States. See https://en.wikipedia.org/wiki/League_of_United_Latin_American_Citizens.
3. American GI Forum was started by Dr. Hector P. Garcia on March 26, 1948, to address the concerns of Mexican American veterans who were segregated from other veteran groups. See https://en.wikipedia.org/wiki/American_GI_Forum.
4. Taken from a 2015 address from Pope Francis to a joint session of Congress.

BIBLIOGRAPHY

Abernethy, Nathan. 1966. "Freshman Law Student Plans to Help People." *Baylor Lariat*, October 18.

Abu-Jamal, Mumia. 2004. *We Want Freedom: A Life in the Black Panther Party*. Cambridge, MA: South End Press.

Acuña, Rodolfo. 1981. *Occupied America: A History of Chicanos*. 2nd ed. New York: Harper & Row.

Adams, James Luther. 1950–51. "Theological Basis for Social Action." *Journal of Religious Thought* 8, no. 1 (Autumn–Winter): 6.

Bean, Alan. 2012. "The Law Falls Silent." *Friends of Justice* (blog), May 11. https://friendsofjustice.wordpress.com.

Bergoglio, Jorge Mario. 2015. Pope Francis Visit 2015. "Address to Joint Meeting of Congress." http://www.popefrancisvisit.com/schedule/address-to-joint-meeting-of-congress/.

Bernstein, Hilda. 1978. *No. 46 Steve Biko*. London: International Defense & Aid Fund.

Berrigan, Phillip. 1970. *Prison Journals of a Revolutionary Priest*. Compiled and edited by Vincent McGee. New York: Ballantine Books.

Boesak, Allan Aubrey. 1977. *Farewell to Innocence: A Socio-Ethical Study of Black Theology and Black Power*. Maryknoll, NY: Orbis Books.

Bonhoeffer, Dietrich. 1967. *The Letters and Papers from Prison.* Translated from the German by Reginald Fuller. New York: The MacMillan, 1967.

Carrillo, Alberto. 1972. "The Chicano and the Church." *IDOC International* (North American Edition): 10.

Carrillo, Alberto. 1971. "The Sociological Failure of the Catholic Church towards the Chicano." *Journal of Mexican Studies* 1, no. 2 (Winter): 75.

Castuera, Ignacio. 1975. "The Theology and Practice of Liberation in the Mexican American Context." *The Perkins School of Theology Journal* 29, no. 1 (Fall): 2.

Católicos por La Raza. 1971. "Demands." *La Raza* 1, no. 1.

Chavarría, Jesús. 1971. "La Causa Chicana: A Revolution Yet to Come." *Origins NC Documentary Service* 4, no. 43: 675.

Chavez, César E. 1975. "Blessed Are You Who Hunger and Thirst for Righteousness, You Shall Be Satisfied." *National Catholic Reporter* 14 (March 7): 14.

Cone, James H. 1970. *A Black Theology of Liberation.* New York: J. B. Lippincott.

Cox, Harvey G. 1973. *The Seduction of the Spirit: The Use and Misuse of Man's Religion.* Simon and Schuster.

"The Del Rio Manifesto to the Nation." 1973. *Maryknoll* 68 (March): 3.

Deloria, Vine J. 1969. *Custer Died for Your Sins: An Indian Manifesto.* New York: Avon Books.

DuBois, W. E. B. 2005. *The Souls of Black Folk.* Bantam Classic, Reissue Ed. New York: Random House, LLC.

Dworkin, Anthony Gary. 1965. "Stereotypes and Self-Image Held by Native-Born and Foreign-Born Mexican-Americans." *Sociology and Social Research* 99 (March–April): 214.

Elizondo, Virgilio P. 1988. *The Future Is Mestizo.* Oak Park, IL: Meyer Stone Books, 1988.

Elizondo, Virgilio P. 1978. *Mestizaje: The Dialectic of Cultural Birth and the Gospel I, II, & III.* San Antonio: Mexican American Cultural Center.

Fanon, Frantz. 1967. *Black Skin, White Masks.* Translated by Charles Lam Markman. New York: Grove Press.

Fanon, Frantz. 1967. *The Wretched of the Earth.* Translated by Constance Farrington. New York: Grove Press.

Freire, Paulo. 1974. *Pedagogy of the Oppressed.* Translated by Myra Bergman Ramos. New York: Seabury Press.

Garcia, Ignacio M. 1989. *Hector P. Garcia: In Relentless Pursuit of Justice.* Houston: Arte Publico Press, 88.

———. 1989. *United We Win: The Rise and Fall of La Raza Unida Party.* Tucson: University of Arizona Press, 56–57.

Gonzáles, Rodolfo. 1972. *I Am Joaquin.* New York: Bantam Books.

Gramsci, Antonio. 1973. *Letters from Prison.* Translated from the Italian and introduced by Lynne Lawner. New York: Harper & Row Publishers.

Guerrero, Andres G. 1987. *A Chicano Theology.* Maryknoll, NY: Orbis Books.

Guevara, Ernesto. 2011. *El Diario del Che en Bolivia.* Edición Autorizada. La Habana, Cuba: Ocean Sur.

Holy Bible. 2011. New International Version, NIV. Biblica, Inc.

Lara-Braud, Jorge. 1969. "The Second Largest Ethnic Minority in the USA." *Migration Today* 12 (Spring): 5.

Magón, Ricardo Flores. 2005. *Dreams of Freedom: A Ricardo Flores Magón Reader.* Edited by Chaz Bufe and Mitchell Cowen Verter. Oakland, CA: AK Press.

Mandela, Nelson. 1979. *I Am Prepared to Die.* London: International Defense Fund for South Africa.

Marquez, Benjamin. 1993. *LULAC: The Evolution of a Mexican American Political Organization.* Chapter 2. Austin: University of Texas Press.

Martí, José. 1987. *Política De Nuestra América.* 5 ed. México, DF: Siglo veintiuno editores, sa.

Martinez, Elizabeth, Ed. 1991. *500 Años del Pueblo Chicano / 500 Years of Chicano History in Pictures.* Albuquerque, NM: SouthWest Organizing Project.

Matthiessen, Peter. 1971. *In the Spirit of Crazy Horse*. New York: Viking Press.

Nabokov, Peter. 1970. *Tijerina and the Courthouse Raid*. Berkeley: Ramparts Press.

Neal, Marie Augusta, SND de N. 1972. "How Prophecy Lives." *Sociological Analysis* 3 (Fall): 125.

Neal, Marie Augusta, SND de N. 1977. *A Socio-Theology of Letting Go*. New York: Paulist Press.

Neihardt, John G. 1975. *Black Elk Speaks*. New York: Pocket Books.

Nieto, Leo D. 1975. "The Chicano Movement and the Churches in the United States." *Perkins School of Theology Journal* 39, no. 1 (Fall): 32.

Nicolai, Georg Friedrich. 1918. *The Biology of War*. New York: The Century Company.

Peltier, Leonard. USP #89637-132. 2000. *Prison Letters: My Life Is My Sundance*. Edited by Harvey Arden. New York: Crazy Horse Spirit, Inc. & Arden Editorial Services.

Ransom, Msgr. Clifton. 2011. *Uncertain Trumpet*. Raleigh, NC: Lulu Enterprises, Inc.

Rendon, Armando. 1971. *A Chicano Manifesto*. New York: Collier Books.

Romero, Juan, and Moises Sandoval. 1975. *Reluctant Dawn: Historia del Padre A. J. Martinez, Cura de Taos*. San Antonio: Mexican American Cultural Center.

Ruskin, John. 1985. *Unto This Last and Other Writings*. New York: Viking Penguin Inc.

Salinas, Raul. 1999. *Un Trip through the Mind Jail y Otras Excursions*. Houston, Texas: Arte Público Press.

Sánchez, Ricardo. 1973. *Canto y grito mi liberación: Y lloro Mis Desmadrazgos*. New York: Anchor Books.

Sandoz, Mari. 1942. *Crazy Horse: The Strange Man of the Ogalas*. Lincoln: University of Nebraska Press.

Sartre, Jean-Paul. 1965. *Anti-Semite and Jew*. Translated by George J. Becker. New York: Schocken Books.

Segundo, Juan L. 1974. *Evolution and Guilt*. Translated by John Drury. Maryknoll, NY: Orbis Books.

Singleton III, Henry H. 2002. *Black Theology and Ideology: Deideological Dimensions in the Theology of James H. Cone*. Collegeville, MN: The Liturgical Press.

Steiner, Stan, and Luis Valdez. 1972. *Aztlan: An Anthology of Mexican American Literature*. New York: Alfred A. Knopf.

Stranger in One's Land. 1970. US Commission on Civil Rights. Clearing House Publication No. 17 (May).

Tijerina, Reies Lopez. 1978. *Mi lucha por la tierra*. Mexico: Fondo de Cultura Económica.

Vasconcelos, José Calderón. 1927. *Indología. Una interpretación de la cultura Ibero-Americana*. Paris: Agencia Mundial de Libreria.

———. 1961. *La Raza Cósmica: Misión de la Raza Ibero-Americana*. Madrid: Aguilar, S.A. Di Ediciones.

Woods, Donald. 1978. *Biko*. New York: Vintage Books.

ABOUT THE AUTHOR

Dr. Andrés G. Guerrero Jr., earned a doctor of applied theology degree from Harvard Divinity School, Cambridge, Massachusetts. He studied at St. Mary's Seminary and the University of St. Thomas, Houston, Texas, and at colleges and universities in Colorado and Mexico. He earned a bachelor's degree in philosophy, an education degree, and several master's degrees in theology and divinity. Guerrero taught in Chicago, Illinois; Saginaw, Michigan; and Greeley, Colorado. Guerrero has four children and five grandchildren.